Scholastic Success With
Traditional Cursive

by Jill Kaufman

S C H O L A S T I C
PROFESSIONAL BOOKS

New York • Toronto • London • Auckland • Sydney •
Mexico City • New Delhi • Hong Kong • Buenos Aires

Scholastic Inc. grants teachers permission to photocopy the reproducible pages from this book for classroom use. No other part of this publication may be reproduced in whole or in part, or stored in a retrieval system, or transmitted in any form or by any means, electronic, mechanical, photocopying, recording, or otherwise without written permission of the publisher. For information regarding permission, write to Scholastic Inc., 557 Broadway, New York, NY 10012.

Cover art by Amy Vangsgard
Cover design by Maria Lilja
Interior illustrations by Mark Mason
Interior design by Quack & Company

ISBN 0-439-44488-8

5 6 7 8 9 10   40   09 08 07 06 05

Scholastic Professional Books

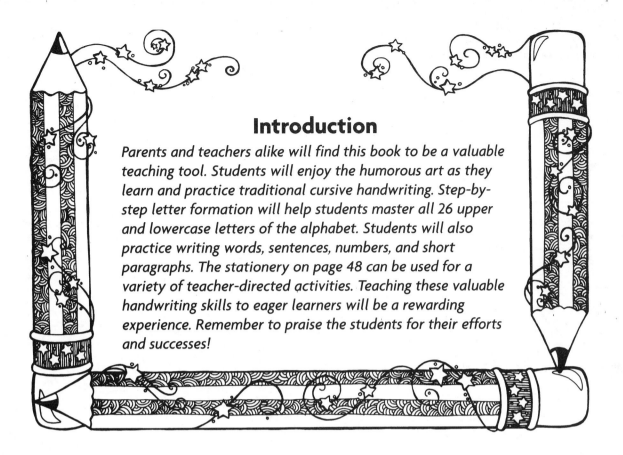

Introduction

Parents and teachers alike will find this book to be a valuable teaching tool. Students will enjoy the humorous art as they learn and practice traditional cursive handwriting. Step-by-step letter formation will help students master all 26 upper and lowercase letters of the alphabet. Students will also practice writing words, sentences, numbers, and short paragraphs. The stationery on page 48 can be used for a variety of teacher-directed activities. Teaching these valuable handwriting skills to eager learners will be a rewarding experience. Remember to praise the students for their efforts and successes!

Table of Contents

A a

Trace and write.

A A

a a

A a

Austin

ant   arid

Al and Ann act

in Australia.

B b

Trace and write.

$\mathcal{B}$ $\mathcal{B}$ $\mathcal{B}$

b b b

$\mathcal{B}$ b $\mathcal{B}$ b

Boise

bib   baby

Bob bakes brownies

in Bakersfield.

Name _____

Cc

Trace and write.

Cc

Cc

Cc

Chicago

city   cute

Christy and Celia

chat in Cancun.

Scholastic Professional Books

Dd

Trace and write.

D D

d d

Dd

Denver

did   dot

Didi and Dad

dive in Dallas.

Ee

Trace and write.

E E

e e

E e

Eugene

eye   each

Emma encountered

Ethan in Egypt.

F f

Trace and write.

$\mathcal{F}$ $\mathcal{F}$

f f

$\mathcal{F}f$ $\mathcal{F}f$

Freeport

fife   file

Frankie frees Fifi

from a fight.

Scholastic Professional Books

Gg

Trace and write.

G   G

g   g

Gg

Glendale

goat   gig

Gabi goes to Greece

to greet Grandpa.

Scholastic Professional Books

Hh

Trace and write.

H H H

h h h

H h

Honolulu

high   hat

Honey, the hamster,

hides in the hedge.

Scholastic Professional Books

Li

Trace and write.

L L L

i i i

Li

Ionia

into   ink

Ida itches in

Indianapolis.

J j

Trace and write.

J J

J j

J j

Joliet

jolt   jest

Jay jumps over

Jack and Jessica.

JACK

JESSICA

JAY

K k

Trace and write.

K K

k k

K k

Kent

kite   keep

King Kirk kicks

in Kenya.

L l

Trace and write.

L L

l l

L l

Lincoln

let's   love

Lee leaves for Lisle

and Louisville.

M m

Trace and write.

m m

m m

M m

Memphis

mom   map

Mia met Mick on

Monday in Mexico.

Name _____

$\mathcal{N}n$

Trace and write.

$\mathcal{N}$ $\mathcal{N}$

n n

$\mathcal{N}n$

$\mathcal{N}orwalk$

$noon$ not

$\mathcal{N}ate\ nibbles\ nuts$

$in\ \mathcal{N}ew\ \mathcal{M}exico.$

Oo

Trace and write.

O O

O O

O O

Olympia

onto   *oil*

Oli and Otis order

Oregon oranges.

OREGON ORANGES

Pp

Trace and write.

P P

p p

Pp

Peoria

pipe *pot*

Peg plays piano

in Pittsburgh.

Scholastic Professional Books

Q q

Trace and write.

Q Q

q q

Q q

Quincy

quiz   quit

Queen Quia quilts

quietly in Quebec.

Scholastic Professional Books

Name _____

Rr

Trace and write.

R R

r r

R r

Reno

roar   rare

Rob rests in Rome

and in Richmond.

Ss

Trace and write.

S S

s s

Ss

St. Louis

sail   sit

Sam and Susan

sing in Seattle.

Tt

Trace and write.

T T

t t

Tt

Tucson

tot   tip

Tita and Timmy

tan in Tahiti.

Uu

Trace and write.

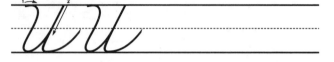

Uu

Urbana

up   utter

Uri used a ukelele

in Uzbekistan.

Scholastic Professional Books

𝒱𝓋

Trace and write.

𝒱𝒱

𝓋 𝓋

𝒱𝓋

Ventura

vase   vote

Vince volunteered

to visit Venezuela.

Ww

Trace and write.

W W

w w

Ww

Westover

wow   wit

Wendy saw Wesley

in Washington, D.C.

Scholastic Professional Books

X x

Trace and write.

X X

x x

X x

Xenia

X-ray   fox

Xavier exited with

six xylophones.

Y y

Trace and write.

Y Y

y y

Y y

Yakima

yard   yet

Yetta and Yuri

visit Yellowstone.

Z z

Trace and write.

Z z

Z z

Z z

Zenda

zip   *zero*

Zeb zigzagged from

Zambia to Zaire.

a-z

A B C D E F

G H I J K L M

N O P Q R S T

U V W X Y Z

Write.

_____

_____

_____

_____

_____

_____

_____

Scholastic Professional Books

Name _____

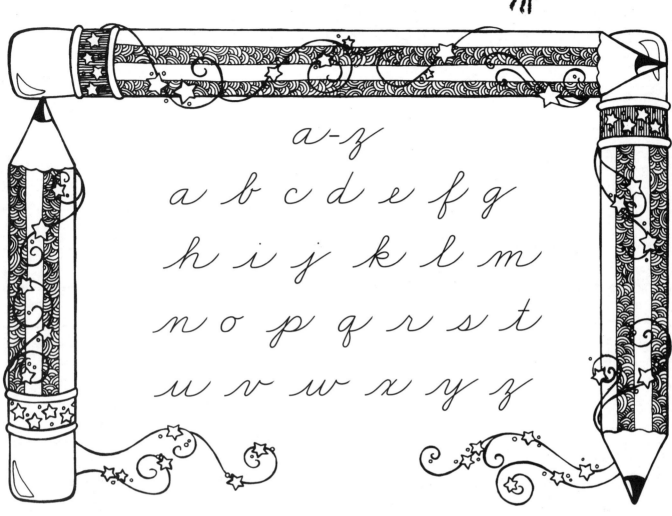

a-z

a b c d e f g

h i j k l m

n o p q r s t

u v w x y z

Write.

_____

- - - - - - - - - - - - - - - - - - -

_____

_____

- - - - - - - - - - - - - - - - - - -

_____

_____

- - - - - - - - - - - - - - - - - - -

_____

_____

- - - - - - - - - - - - - - - - - - -

_____

Numbers 0-9

Trace and write.

0 0 _____

1 1 _____

2 2 _____

3 3 _____

4 4 _____

5 5 _____

6 6 _____

7 7 _____

8 8 _____

9 9 _____

Electing Our President

Presidential elections are held every four years. In 1951, the 22nd Amendment to the Constitution was approved. It says that no one may be elected president more than twice. William Harrison was president for only one month. Franklin Delano Roosevelt was president for 12 years, one month, and eight days.

Write.

_____
_____
_____
_____
_____
_____
_____
_____
_____
_____
_____
_____
_____
_____
_____

Our Presidents

The presidents of the United States have differed from one another in many ways. Some were tall. Some were short. Some were fat. Some were thin. Some were young. Some were old. All of them, however, loved their country and wanted to serve it well.

Write.

_____

_____

_____

_____

_____

_____

_____

_____

_____

_____

_____

_____

_____

_____

_____

_____

_____

Teeth Talk

President George Washington wore false teeth. His false teeth were made of elephant and walrus tusk, cow, hippo, and human teeth. Washington had his horses' teeth brushed every morning.

Write.

Name _____

A Bit Plump

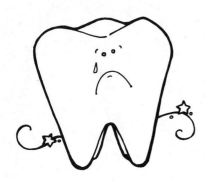

Like Washington, John Adams had lost nearly all his teeth. Unlike Washington, he refused to have false teeth. Adams was on the plump side. That is why his opponents nicknamed him "His Rotundity."

Write.

_____
- -
_____
- -
_____
- -
_____
- -
_____
- -
_____
- -
_____
- -
_____
- -
_____
- -
_____
- -

Not a Day to Celebrate

Three of the first five presidents died on the 4th of July. They were John Adams, Thomas Jefferson, and James Monroe. Adams and Jefferson died in the same year. Supposedly Jefferson's last words were "Is it the 4th?"

Write.

_____

_____

_____

_____

_____

_____

_____

_____

_____

_____

_____

_____

_____

_____

Name _____

The Bear Facts

Thomas Jefferson sent Lewis and
Clark to explore the new territory.
They returned with hundreds of
plant and animal samples
including two grizzly bears. The
bears lived in cages on the grounds
of the White House.

Write.

_____

_____
_ _
_____

_____
_ _
_____

_____
_ _
_____

_____
_ _
_____

_____
_ _
_____

_____
_ _
_____

Name _____

A Long Speech

    William Henry Harrison gave the longest inaugural address in the history of the presidency. It lasted almost two hours. The weather was cold and rainy. Harrison caught a cold and died 31 days later of pneumonia.

Write.

_____

_____

_____

_____

_____

_____

_____

_____

_____

_____

_____

_____

_____

_____

_____

Scholastic Professional Books

Name _____

Pool, Anyone?

John Quincy Adams brought two new things to the White House. He brought a pool table and his pet alligator. Adams was the first president whose father was also president.

Write.

_____
- -
_____
- -
_____
- -
_____
- -
_____
- -
_____
- -
_____
- -
_____
- -
_____

A Family Man

John Tyler had 15 children—
the most of any president. Legend
has it that he was playing
marbles with his little boys
when he found out he was
president. He often gave parties at
the White House for his children
and grandchildren.

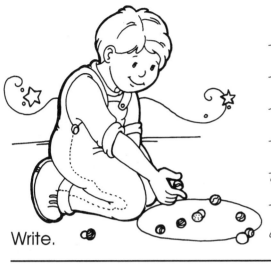

Write.

A President's Request

Andrew Johnson requested that when he died, he wanted to be wrapped in an American flag. He also wanted a copy of the United States Constitution placed under his head. Both of Johnson's wishes were granted.

Write.

_____

_____

_____

_____

_____

_____

_____

_____

_____

_____

Name _____

Can You Imagine?

William Howard Taft was our heaviest president. He weighed in at 332 pounds. He once got stuck in a bathtub at the White House. Despite Taft's large size, he was a good baseball player.

Write.

_____
- -
_____
- -
_____
- -
_____
- -
_____
- -
_____
- -
_____
- -
_____
- -
_____
- -
_____
- -

Very Tall

At six feet four inches, Abraham Lincoln was our tallest president. He seemed even taller because he always wore a tall silk hat. Lincoln kept his important papers under his hat so he would not lose them!

Write.

_____

_____

_____

_____

_____

_____

_____

_____

_____

_____

_____

_____

_____

_____

_____

_____

_____

Name _____

A Real Star

Only one president was a movie star before he was elected—Ronald Reagan. He had acted in more than 50 movies. Reagan was our oldest elected president. He kept a jar of jelly beans on his desk.

Write.

_____
_____
_____
_____
_____
_____
_____
_____
_____
_____
_____
_____
_____
_____

Batter Up!

While growing up, George W. Bush's dream was to be a major-league baseball player. He never made it, but he did become president. President Bush has a collection of 250 signed baseballs.

Write.

_____

_____

_____

_____

_____

_____

_____

_____

_____

_____

Scholastic Professional Books

A Love of Books

Several of the presidents had a love of reading. Thomas Jefferson said he could not live without books. Abraham Lincoln often borrowed books from his neighbors. By the time Harry Truman was 15, he had read every book in the town library!

Write.